AMAZING BRAIN

Mick Gowar

OXFORD
UNIVERSITY PRESS

OXFORD
UNIVERSITY PRESS

is a department of the University of Oxford.
It furthers the University's objective of excellence in research, scholarship,
and education by publishing worldwide in

Oxford   New York

Auckland   Cape Town   Dar es Salaam   Hong Kong   Karachi
Kuala Lumpur   Madrid   Melbourne   Mexico City   Nairobi
New Delhi   Shanghai   Taipei   Toronto

With offices in

Argentina   Austria   Brazil   Chile   Czech Republic   France   Greece
Guatemala   Hungary   Italy   Japan   Poland   Portugal   Singapore
South Korea   Switzerland   Thailand   Turkey   Ukraine   Vietnam

British Library Cataloguing in Publication Data

Data available

ISBN: 978-0-19-846105-0

9 10 8

Printed in China

Paper used in the production of this book is a natural,
recyclable product made from wood grown in sustainable forests.
The manufacturing process conforms to the environmental
regulations of the country of origin

Acknowledgements

The publisher would like to thank the following for permission to reproduce photographs:
p5 Dejan Kostic/Alamy; **p8** Eye Of Science/Science Photo Library; **p14** AKG – Images;
p18 Michael Brennan/Corbis UK Ltd.; **p19** Everynight Images/Alamy; **p20** Lester Lefkowitz/Corbis
UK Ltd.; **p21** Annabella Bluesky/Science Photo Library

Cover: Corbis/Michael Freeman

Illustrations by Maurizo de Angelis/Beehive Illustration: **p4**, **p6**r, **p9**, **p12/13**, **p17**, **p18**, **p22/23**;
Jess Mikhail: **p6**t, b, **p7**, **p10/11**, **p15**, **p16**

Contents

Amazing brain

This book is about your amazing brain.

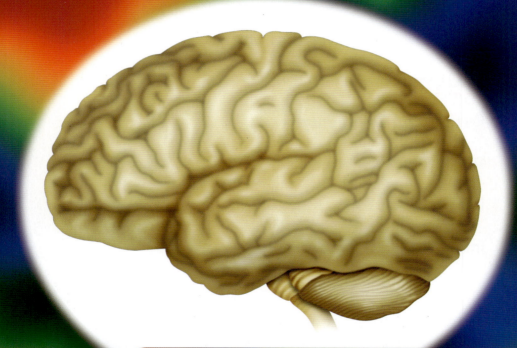

This is a picture of a brain. It looks like a wrinkled jelly and it only weighs as much as a bag of sugar, but without your brain no other part of your body could work. Your brain makes sense of everything you see, hear, smell, touch and taste, and it controls all the muscles in your body.

This is a police control centre. It's 'the brain' of the police force. Pictures come along cables into the centre from CCTV cameras all over town.
The pictures are then shown on the big screens.
If the officers in the control centre see something suspicious happening on one of the screens they can send a car or foot patrol to investigate. Police officers in patrol cars and on foot also report to the control centre by radio. They can ask for extra help from the officers in the control centre.

Your brain is the control centre of your body.

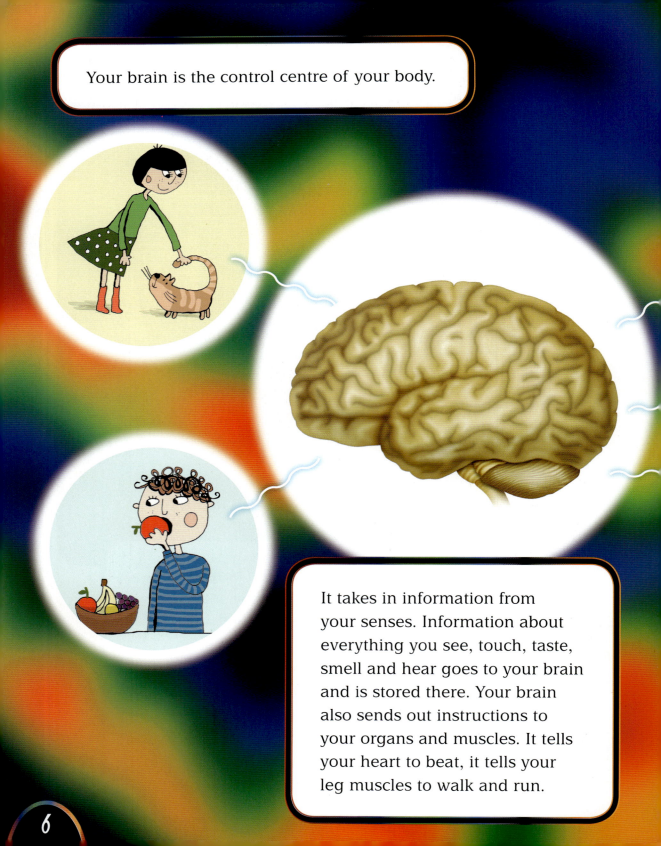

It takes in information from your senses. Information about everything you see, touch, taste, smell and hear goes to your brain and is stored there. Your brain also sends out instructions to your organs and muscles. It tells your heart to beat, it tells your leg muscles to walk and run.

Your brain is in charge of everything. If your muscles and organs didn't have your brain to tell them what to do, they would stop working.

A STORY ABOUT BRAINS!

Brain fact

You were born with approximately 100,000 million brain cells. Like all the other cells that make up your body, brain cells need food, water and oxygen or they will die. You lose millions of brain cells every year. But don't worry. Scientists have recently discovered that you grow new brain cells just when you need them most – in your teens and twenties when you are taking important exams!

Information in/ instructions out

All the messages going to your brain from your senses travel along chains of linked cells called nerves. Like telephone wires carrying broadband Internet, a huge amount of information is travelling along the nerves all the time. Nerves also carry all the instructions that are going out from your brain to your organs and muscles.

Brain cells, grown in a culture. Top left is a large nerve cell body.

Nerves carry information to and from every part of your body, but they join up in the spinal cord. The spinal cord is a huge bundle of nerves running inside your backbone. It is like a motorway, taking all the traffic or information into your brain, and taking all the orders out to the muscles and organs.

Brain fact

There are 150,000 kilometres of nerves in your body. If you laid them out straight, these nerves would be long enough to go all the way round the world more than three times.

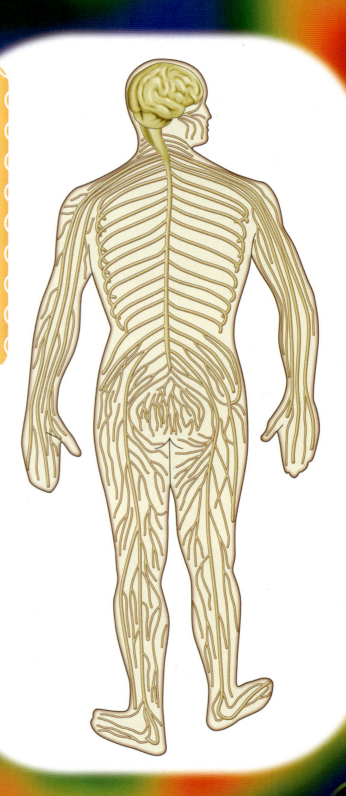

Here's an example of how your nervous system works.

Eyes to brain: I can see lots of black dots and squiggles on a white sheet.

Memory: It's music. These are the notes you are going to play. The first note is B.

Brain to arm and hand:
- Arm muscles – some of you tighten and some of you relax so the hands can get in the right position
- Left thumb – you cover the hole on the back of the recorder
- Left index finger – you cover the top hole.

Brain to mouth:
- Lips – you tighten around the mouthpiece
- Lungs – breathe in and blow, but not too hard

It can take less than one second for your brain to take in all that information and send out all those instructions.

Brain tester

Try this simple test to see how fast messages travel from your eye to your brain and then from your brain to your muscles. You will need a ruler.

1 Ask a friend to hold the ruler vertically.

2 Place the thumb and forefinger of one of your hands either side of the ruler, but don't touch it.

3 Your friend should now let go of the ruler without warning you.

4 Catch the ruler between your thumb and forefinger before it hits the ground.

You can use the scale on the ruler to measure how quick you are. Now, swap over and test your friend.

Inside your brain

Let's take a closer look at a brain and see which part does what.

This is the **cerebrum** and it's the largest part of your brain. It's the part you think with and it helps you to read, write and do maths. It's also the part of your brain you use to solve puzzles and problems. All your memories are stored in your cerebrum, and it also controls your behaviour.

The **cerebellum** is like the autopilot in a plane. Once you've learnt to do something physical – like walking or riding a bicycle – your cerebellum can take over control from the thinking part of your brain and make the actions automatic. That means you can walk or run without having to think all the time about having to put one foot in front of the other. It also makes sure you keep your balance.

At the top of your **spinal cord** is your brain stem. It's only about 7.5 cm long, but it's the part of the brain that keeps you alive, because it's the part that controls your heart, your breathing and digestion. It's also where the most mysterious things happen, because it's where your dreams are created.

People used to believe that dreams were signs of what would happen in the future.

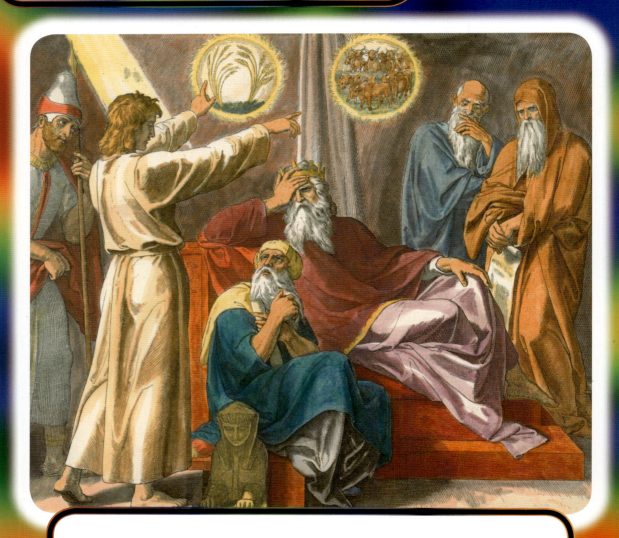

Joseph became one of the most important men in Egypt because he claimed to understand the meanings of dreams. Joseph told the Pharaoh that his dreams foretold a great famine, but they also showed what the Pharaoh should do to prevent his people from starving.

An Austrian psychiatrist called Sigmund Freud thought dreams gave away our secret thoughts and worries. He said that:

Dreaming you're running away from a monster that's chasing you shows that you're really running away from a problem. It's telling you that you need to do something about it.

If you dream you're falling it means you're worrying – perhaps about a test in school or something you've done wrong.

If you dream you're flying it means you're confident and happy.

Ouch! Help! Emergency!

Wouldn't it be great if you didn't feel pain? Imagine: no more toothache; no more pain from wasps or nettles. Actually, it wouldn't be great. Pain is a warning signal that something is wrong or you are in danger.

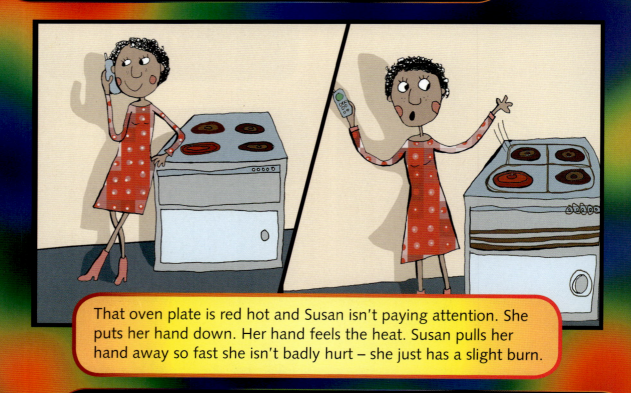

That oven plate is red hot and Susan isn't paying attention. She puts her hand down. Her hand feels the heat. Susan pulls her hand away so fast she isn't badly hurt – she just has a slight burn.

In fact, Susan moved her hand faster than the speed of thought!

What saved her from being burned was a reflex.

Normally, it takes 0.8 seconds for a message to go from your finger to your brain and to get an instruction back. In that time Susan's hand would have been badly burned.

Because Susan was in great danger the message didn't go to her brain at all. It went to her spinal chord and back again which is a much shorter journey. That emergency instruction, which is automatic, is called a reflex and it only took 0.03 seconds.

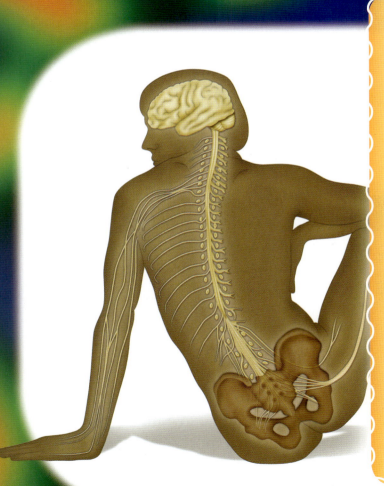

Brain fact

Some other reflexes include:

- **Blinking (blinking reflex) – when something comes towards your eye, like a fly**
- **Gagging (gagging reflex) – when something tickles the back of your throat**
- **Sneezing (sneezing reflex) – when something irritates the lining inside your nose**
- **Putting your hands in front of your face if a ball or some other object comes towards you.**

When things go wrong

Concussion

Even though your skull is a great protection for your brain, injuries can happen. The commonest brain injury is concussion. It's caused when the brain is shaken violently and hits the inside of the skull.

This can happen when a person:

- receives a blow to the head

- has been shaken very hard

- has been in a car crash, for example, and their head has been thrown forward or backwards very suddenly.

Concussion can cause unconsciousness and can make someone feel confused and sick. Some people may even lose their memory for a short time.

The good news is that people suffering from concussion get better fairly quickly without any lasting damage to the brain. Repeated blows to the head can, however, cause much more serious damage. That's why many doctors would like the sport of boxing to be banned.

Epilepsy

Epilepsy is caused by a fault in the brain's communication system, when so many messages are hurtling around the brain that the body can't cope with them. The result is a seizure or fit, in which:

- the person may lose their balance

- their limbs may begin to twitch

- they may lose consciousness.

No one knows the exact cause of epilepsy, but sometimes extreme tiredness or flashing lights can trigger a seizure.

Depression

Depression is a disease of the mind. It's more than feeling sad, it's feeling so ill and miserable that you can't live a normal life. It's a serious illness that needs treatment like any other illness.

Who can help?

Neurologist and neurosurgeon

'Neuro' means to do with nerves and the brain. A neurologist is a doctor who treats injuries and diseases of the brain and nervous system. For example, if someone has epilepsy or has a head injury they will be treated by a neurologist. If they need an operation, this will be done by a neurosurgeon.

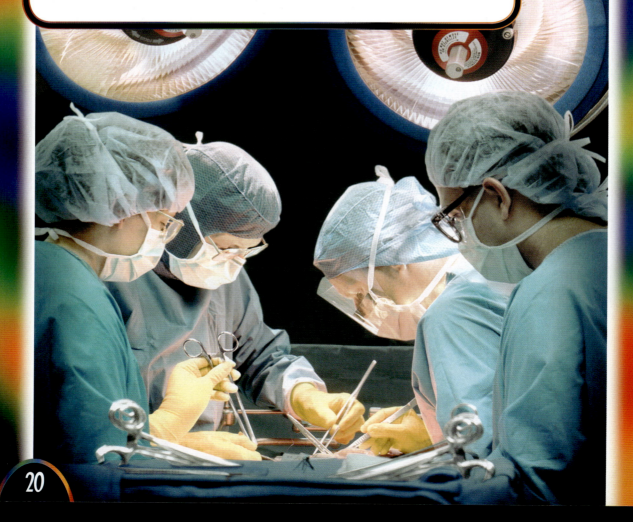

Psychiatrist

'Psyche' is a Greek word meaning 'soul' or 'mind'. Doctors who treat people with diseases of the mind and emotions, like depression, are called psychiatrists. They will treat the disease with special drugs and also by helping patients to talk about how they feel. Sometimes encouraging patients to talk about their feelings can help them as much as giving them medication.

Psychologist

Psychologists are scientists who study the human mind – they are not medical doctors. They are interested in how the mind works and why people behave as they do. They do experiments to see how quickly people can do tests like mental maths puzzles or how quickly people learn new things.

This pyschologist is watching a child do a puzzle.

Finally, let's find out how many different parts of your brain are needed to help you do a really complicated task like reading this page.

Brain stem: sends the orders that tell your heart to beat and your lungs to breathe. Without those things happening, you wouldn't be able to read at all because you wouldn't be alive!

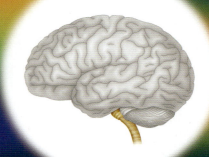

Cerebellum: helps you keep your balance so you can sit in your chair without falling over, and hold the book without dropping it. That's important.

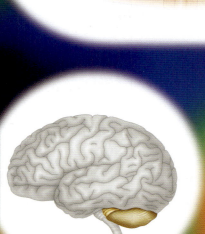

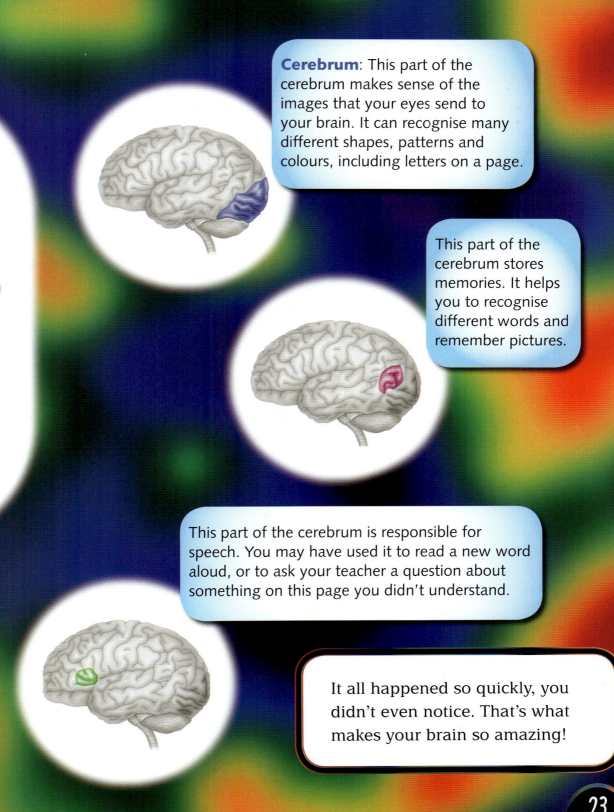

Cerebrum: This part of the cerebrum makes sense of the images that your eyes send to your brain. It can recognise many different shapes, patterns and colours, including letters on a page.

This part of the cerebrum stores memories. It helps you to recognise different words and remember pictures.

This part of the cerebrum is responsible for speech. You may have used it to read a new word aloud, or to ask your teacher a question about something on this page you didn't understand.

It all happened so quickly, you didn't even notice. That's what makes your brain so amazing!

Index

Quiz

1. How many brain cells did you have when you were born?
   i) 100,000
   ii) 100 million
   iii) 100,000 million

2. What does "neuro" mean?
   i) contains water
   ii) to do with nerves and the brain
   iii) runs on atomic power

3. What does a psychiatrist treat?
   i) brain and spinal injuries
   ii) diseases of the mind, like depression
   iii) diseases of the eye

4. How many kilometres of nerves are in your body?
   i) 1,500
   ii) 150,000
   iii) 150 million

5. Which part of your brain controls balance?
   i) cerebrum
   ii) cerebellum
   iii) brain stem

Where to find the answers:
1. p7; **2**. p20; **3**. p21;
4. p9; **5**. p13